PRAYING IN THE PRESENCE OF

OUR LORD

D1115211

PRAYING IN THE PRESENCE

OF

OUR LORD

PRAYERS FOR EUCHARISTIC ADORATION

FR. BENEDICT J. GROESCHEL, C.F.R.

Our Sunday Visitor Publishing Division
Our Sunday Visitor, Inc.
Huntington, Indiana 46750

Nihil Obstat: Francis J. McAree, S.T.D.
Censor Librorum
Imprimatur: ✠ Patrick J. Sheridan, D.D.
Vicar General, Archdiocese of New York
January 11, 1999

The *Nihil Obstat* and *Imprimatur* are official declarations that a book or pamphlet is free of doctrinal or moral error. No implication is contained therein that those who have granted the *Nihil Obstat* and *Imprimatur* agree with the contents, opinions, or statements expressed.

The author and publisher are grateful to those publishers and others whose material, whether in the public domain or protected by copyright laws and cited throughout, have been included in this work. If any copyrighted materials have been inadvertently used in this book without proper credit being given in one manner or another, please notify Our Sunday Visitor in writing so that future printings of this work may be corrected accordingly.

Copyright © 1999 by Our Sunday Visitor Publishing Division,
Our Sunday Visitor Inc.

All rights reserved. With the exception of short excerpts for critical reviews, no part of this work may be reproduced in any manner whatsoever without permission in writing from the publisher. Write:
Our Sunday Visitor Publishing Division
Our Sunday Visitor, Inc.
200 Noll Plaza
Huntington, IN 46750

ISBN: 978-087973-586-9 (Inventory No. 586)
eISBN: 978-1-61278-354-3
LCCCN: 98-68199

Cover photo by John Zierten
Cover design by Tyler Ottinger

PRINTED IN THE UNITED STATES OF AMERICA

FOR ALL WHO HAVE TAUGHT
OR NOW TEACH US TO
KNOW AND LOVE CHRIST IN
THE HOLY EUCHARIST

Acknowledgements

We are grateful to those publishers and authors who have given us permission to excerpt materials from their works. Among them are: The Vatican Press, which provided the translations of the encyclicals cited, as they appear in *The Encyclicals of John Paul II*, by J. Michael Miller, C.S.B., © 1996 by Our Sunday Visitor Publishing Division; ICS Publications, *Story of a Soul*, translated by John Clarke, O.C.D, © 1975, 1976 by the Washington Province of Discalced Carmelite Friars Publications; *L'Osservatore Romano*, English edition; the Catholic Book Publishing Co., *The Way of Salvation*, translated from the Italian of St. Alphonsus de Liguori, © 1948, and the *Enchiridion of Indulgences*, translated by William T. Barry, C.SS.R, © 1968; Paulist Press, *The Prayers of Catherine of Siena*, by Sister Suzanne Noffke, O.P., © 1983; Creative Communications for the Parish, *Sacrament Most Holy: Prayers to Christ in the Eucharist*, by Father Benedict J. Groeschel, C.F.R., © 1997; the Franciscan Friars of the Immaculate, *Jesus Our Eucharistic Love*, by Father Stefano M. Manelli, F.I., © 1996; Burns and Oates, *Ancient Devotions for Holy Communion*, © 1948, used with permission of Burns and Oates; Sophia Institute Press, *Devoutly I Adore Thee: The Prayers and Hymns of St. Thomas Aquinas*, translated and edited by Robert Anderson and Johann Moser, © 1993, and *Preparing Yourself for Mass*, by Romano Guardini, © 1939 Matthias Gruenewald Verlay, English translation, © 1993; the Confraternity of the Precious Blood, *My Imitation of Christ: Revised*, by Thomas á Kempis, translated by the Confraternity, © 1954 and used with permission; Alba House, Society of St. Paul, *Meditations on Mary: Conferences by the Servant of God Terence Cardinal Cooke*, by Cardinal Cooke, © 1993; *Prayers and Devotions from Pope John XXIII, by Pope John XXIII*, copyright © 1984 by The K.S. Giniger Company, Inc. Used by permission of Viking Penguin, a division of Penguin Group (USA) Inc.; Glencoe McGraw-Hill, *Roman Breviary in English: Autumn*, edited by Monsignor Joseph Nelson, D.D., © 1950; Libreria Editrice Vaticana, *Mystery of Faith: Mysterium Fidei,* © 1965; and Alcuin Club and Cassell/Mowbray, *The Sarum Missal in English*, © 1911, 1913, reproduced with permission.

Scripture citations are taken from the *Revised Standard Bible, Catholic Edition*, © 1965 and 1966 by the Division of Christian Education of the National Council of the Churches of Christ in the U.S.A., and are used by permission of the copyright holder. All rights reserved.

Table of Contents

Foreword

A few years ago, I promised to put together a book of prayers to Christ present in the Eucharist. I was working with James Monti at the time on our book, *In the Presence of Our Lord*. James and I collected very beautiful Eucharistic prayers, and I have selected some of them. Interspersed with these prayers are a few I composed myself for a small booklet of Eucharistic prayers published by Creative Communications for the Parish. These are included because they are more contemporary and use language more familiar to the present-day reader. All of these prayers are meant for slow, meditative praying rather than quick recital. I am deeply grateful to James for his essential help in this endeavor, and both of us hope and pray that this little book will contribute to the great renewal in Eucharistic piety we see taking place on the eve of the third millennium.

Fr. Benedict J. Groeschel, C.F.R.
St. Crispin's Friary, Bronx, N.Y.
Feast of St. Francis, 1998

Introduction

... When [St. Teresa] heard people say they wished they had lived when Christ walked on this earth, she would smile to herself, for she knew that we have Him as truly with us in the Most Holy Sacrament as people had Him then, and wonder what more they could possibly want.

— St. Teresa of Ávila, *The Way of Perfection*[1]

Christ promised to be with us, His followers, till the end of the ages. He is present to us in many ways — He is present by His divine power as Word of God through whom all things are made. He is present in the words of Scripture, especially the Gospels. He is present where two or three are gathered in His name. He is present in the poor, the hungry, the stranger, even the imprisoned.

But in a singular way He is present in the sacraments — His mysterious signs, as they were first called — pledges of His saving and sanctifying grace. He comes to us in Baptism to save, in Reconciliation to forgive, and in Matrimony to bless the home. He strengthens the sick, prepares the dying, and ordains His ministers — bishops, priests, and deacons.

But in the Holy Eucharist He comes to draw us

into the most intimate participation in the Paschal Mystery of salvation — into His holy life and work. His death and resurrection are proclaimed and recalled — and we are fed with the Bread of Life, all because He is present, not only in His Soul and Divinity but in His Body and Blood. He is present not only as Son of God, but likewise as Son of Man, Son of Mary. He is here as Jesus of Nazareth.

The Fathers of the early Church, who taught and explained the faith in their sermons and writings, proclaimed Christ's real presence in the Eucharist. In the Mass He was always welcomed and adored as King and Savior. In the fifth century Saint Augustine claimed that not to adore Christ in the Eucharist by some external sign of reverence was a sin. Saint John Chrysostom said that He is even here with us in His robe and sandals. The Church invites you to adore Him in His Eucharistic presence as a continuation of His presence in the Mass.[2]

Since perhaps as early as the sixth century devout people have adored Christ's presence in the Holy Eucharist which was kept for the communion of the sick.[3] By the thirteenth century, especially because of the preaching of Saint Francis, devout Christians had found in the Eucharist a most profound way to reverence the presence of Christ Jesus in their lives.[4] Since that time every canonized saint and millions of devout people have found the most profound consolation, reassurance, and challenge to grow in faith, hope, and charity before the Tabernacle. This little book is meant to introduce those who are unfamiliar or sadly uninformed to this crown jewel of Catholic devotion and to lead them to a prayerful knowledge of Christ through a collection of prayers that great Christians have said before the Eucharist from ancient to modern times.

Please note: All prayers marked with the initials "BJG" are from my booklet, *Sacrament Most Holy: Prayers to Christ in the Eucharist*, published by Creative Communications for the Parish, St. Louis, Missouri, 1997.

Prayers Before and After Mass

The celebration of the Holy Eucharist, also called the Liturgy or Mass, is the preeminent public act of worship of the Christian people. However, we will profit much spiritually if we are well prepared before Mass and pause to recollect afterwards about what has happened to us. What better way to do this than to lift up our minds and hearts to Christ — present with us as He was in Bethlehem, Nazareth, Jerusalem, and as He is now in eternal life — God and man, divine and human?

From a Conference of the Servant of God Terence Cardinal Cooke
(1921-1983)
Archbishop of New York

The spiritual energy, the grace which comes with each reception of Holy Communion, we absorb only in proportion to our dispositions at the time we receive. Again, some proportion exists between our preparation and thanksgiving for Holy Communion and the grace we receive from the Blessed Sacrament. A hunger and thirst for union with our Divine Lord will result in a good preparation and thanksgiving. Sometimes we start our preparation for Holy Communion with no very great longing for union with our Lord, but our preparation results in an increased desire for him. Here preparation becomes the cause of our longing for union with our Divine Savior. Ordinarily it is the effect of an intense desire to be united with him and to be less unworthy of this union by reason of our preparation. From experience we learn that little or no desire for Holy Communion will result in no preparation or only a minimum of preparation. In return, we should not be surprised to receive from the Blessed Sacrament only a minimum of divine grace.

In this matter, as in all other matters, God has given us free will. He will not force us to prepare to receive him. He will not force us to thank him for his unspeakable gift after we have received. Even God's grace does not take away our free will, nor does it perform miracles. The grace of God operates when, and only when, we cooperate with it....

Let us beg of God the grace to hunger and thirst for Holy Communion. Through Mary's intercession, let us ask for the spiritual help to make better preparations and thanksgivings. On our part, let us determine to cooperate with the operations of grace constantly taking place in our soul.[5]

MEDITATION OF ST. FRANCIS OF ASSISI

Let everyone be struck with fear,
the whole world tremble,
and the heavens exult
when Christ, the Son of the living God,
is present on the altar in the hands of a priest!
O wonderful loftiness
and stupendous dignity!
O sublime humility!
O humble sublimity!
The Lord of the universe,
God and the Son of God,
so humbles Himself
that He hides Himself
for our salvation
under an ordinary piece of bread!

See the humility of God, brothers,
and *pour out your hearts before Him* (Ps. 62:8
    [V 61:9])!
Humble yourselves
that you may be exalted by Him (cf. 1 Pet. 5:6;
    Jas 4:10)!
Hold back nothing of yourselves for yourselves,
that He Who gives Himself totally to you
may receive you totally![6]

19

PRAYER FOR FREQUENT COMMUNION

FROM THE IMITATION OF CHRIST BY THOMAS À KEMPIS
(CA. 1380-1471)

Behold, I come to Thee, O Lord, that it may be well with me by Thy gift, and that I may be delighted in Thy holy banquet, which "in Thy sweetness, O God, Thou hast provided for the poor" (Ps. LXVII. 11).

Behold, in Thee is all whatsoever I can or ought to desire; Thou art my salvation and redemption, my hope and my strength, my honor and my glory.

Therefore, "give joy to the soul of Thy servant, for to Thee, this day, O Lord Jesus, I have lifted up my soul" (Ps. LXXXV. 4).

I desire at this time to receive Thee devoutly and reverently; I would gladly bring Thee into my house, that, like Zacheus, I may receive Thy blessing, and be numbered among the children of Abraham (Lk. XIX. 9).

My soul longs to be nourished with Thy Body; my heart desires to be united with Thee.

Give Thyself to me and it is enough; for without Thee no comfort is availing.

Without Thee I cannot subsist; and without Thy visitation I cannot live.

And, therefore, I must come often to Thee, and receive Thee for the remedy, and for the health and strength of my soul; lest perhaps I faint in the way, if I be deprived of this heavenly food.

For so, O most merciful Jesus, Thou wast pleased once to say, when Thou hadst been preaching to the people, and curing various diseases: "I will not send them away fasting, lest they faint in the way" (Mt. XV. 32).

Deal now in like manner with me, who hast left Thyself in the sacrament for the comfort of Thy faithful.

For Thou art the most sweet refection of the soul; and he that shall eat Thee worthily shall be partaker and heir of everlasting glory.

It is indeed necessary for me, who so often fall and commit sin, and so quickly grow slack and faint, by frequent prayers and confessions, and by the holy communion of Thy Body, to repair my strength, to cleanse and inflame my soul, lest perhaps by abstaining for a longer time, I fall away from my holy purpose.

For the imaginations of man are prone to evil from his youth (Gn. VIII. 21); and unless Thy divine medicine succor him man quickly becomes worse.

The Holy Communion, therefore, withdraws him from evil, and strengthens him in good.

But if I am so often negligent and lukewarm now

when I communicate, or celebrate, how would it be were I not to take this remedy, and seek so great a help?

And although I am not every day fit nor well disposed to celebrate, yet I will endeavor, at proper times, to receive the divine mysteries, and to make myself partaker of so great a grace.

For this is the one main comfort of a faithful soul, so long as she sojourns afar off from Thee in this mortal body; being mindful often of her God, to receive her beloved with a devout mind.

O wonderful condescension of Thy tender love towards us, that Thou, O Lord God, the Creator and enlivener of all spirits, shouldst vouchsafe to come to a poor soul, and with Thy whole divinity and humanity, satisfy her hunger!

O happy mind, and blessed soul, which deserves to receive Thee, her Lord God, devoutly; and in receiving Thee, to be filled with spiritual joy!

Oh, how great a Lord does she entertain! how beloved a guest does she bring into her house! how sweet a companion does she receive! how faithful a friend does she welcome! how beautiful and how noble a spouse does she embrace, beloved above all, and to be loved beyond all that she can desire!

Let heaven and earth, with all their attire, be silent in Thy presence, O my dearest beloved (Heb. II. 20); for whatever praise or beauty they have is all the gift of Thy bounty; nor can they equal the beauty of Thy name, of whose wisdom there is no end.[7]

FROM THE WRITINGS OF MONSIGNOR ROMANO GUARDINI
(1885-1968)

The memorial which the Lord bequeathed us is not merely the memory of an event or the portrayal of a great figure; it is the fulfillment of our personal relation to Christ, of the believer to his Redeemer. In the Mass, Christ comes in all His personal reality, bearing His salutary destiny. He comes not just to anyone, but to His own....

... In Communion, He approaches each of us individually and says: "Behold, I stand at the door and Knock" (Apoc. 3:20). Insofar as the "door" swings open in genuine faith and love, He enters and gives Himself to the believer for his own....

To wait for Him, to invite Him, to go to receive and honor and praise Him, to be with Him, drawn into the intimacy of Communion with Him — that is the Christian feast.[8]

BEFORE MASS

FROM THE WRITINGS OF
BISHOP JACOB APHRAATES (FOURTH CENTURY)
FATHER OF THE CHURCH AND SYRIAC MONK

For there is only one door to thy house which is the temple of God.... Therefore let a man watch carefully over his mouth into which the King's Son enters, in that he fast in abstinence from all sins, and so receive the Body and Blood of the Lord.[9]

PRAYER OF ST. PASCHAL BAYLON
(1540-1592)
FRANCISCAN LAY BROTHER AND EUCHARISTIC PATRON

King of the heavens, my Lord Jesus Christ, I an unworthy sinner approach your holy altar, invited by your divine voice, and relying on your mercy. You call me to your table, offering yourself to me for food: therefore, although a child, I will venture as a second Benjamin to come to the banquet which my elder Joseph prepared for his brothers. I entreat your Majesty, may I bring back from there its fruits which so sublime a Sacrament works in your friends. I am infirm, you the Doctor of my salvation. I am a sinner, you are He who justifies the impious. I am poor, you rich in infinite riches. Give to me an increase of faith, an increase of love, a complement of all virtues, with which I may serve you, I may praise you all my life, that at last I may enjoy you in heaven.... Amen.[10]

THE CHERUBIC HYMN
FROM THE BYZANTINE LITURGY

Let us, who mystically represent the Cherubim, and sing the thrice-holy hymn to the life-creating Trinity, now set aside all earthly cares. That we may welcome the King of all, invisibly escorted by angelic hosts. Alleluia, Alleluia, Alleluia![11]

PRAYER OF VENERABLE
JOHN HENRY NEWMAN
(1801-1890)

O my God, holiness becometh Thy House, and yet Thou dost make Thy abode in my breast. My Lord, my Saviour, to me Thou comest, hidden under the semblance of earthly things, yet in that very flesh and blood which Thou didst take from Mary. Thou, who didst

25

first inhabit Mary's breast, dost come to me. My God, Thou seest me; I cannot see myself.... Thou seest how unworthy so great a sinner is to receive the One Holy God, whom the Seraphim adore with trembling....

My God, enable me to bear Thee, for Thou alone canst. Cleanse my heart and mind from all that is past.... Give me a true perception of things unseen, and make me truly, practically, and in the details of life, prefer Thee to anything on earth, and the future world to the present.[12]

PRAYER ATTRIBUTED TO ST. JOHN CHRYSOSTOM
(347-407)
ARCHBISHOP OF CONSTANTINOPLE AND FATHER OF THE CHURCH

I know, O Lord my God, that I am not worthy nor sufficient that You should come under the roof of my soul's habitation, for it is all deserted and in ruins, and You have not in me where worthily to lay Your head. But as from the height of Your glory You did humble Yourself for us, bear now also with my lowliness; and as You did deign to lay Yourself down in a manger in a cave, so deign now also to enter into the manger of my sinful soul and defiled body; and as You did not refuse to enter into the house of Simon the leper and to sup there with sinners, so also deign to enter into the habitation of my humble soul, leprous and sinful; and as You did not reject the sinful woman who approached and touched You, so also have pity on me, a sinner, coming to You and touching You. And grant that I may partake of Your precious Body and Blood to the sanctification, enlightenment, and strengthening of my humble soul and body, to the alleviation of the burden of my many sins, to my preservation from all the snares of the devil, to victory over my sinful and evil habits, to the mortification of my passions, to the fulfillment of Your commandments, to the increase of Your divine grace, and to the inheritance of Your kingdom. For it is not in lightness of heart, O Christ my God, that I venture to approach You, but trusting in Your infinite goodness, and in the fear that being drawn afar from You I may become the prey of our spiritual enemy. Therefore do I pray unto You, O Lord, who alone are holy, that You would sanctify my soul and body, my heart and mind, and, renewing me entirely, would implant in my members the fear of You. And be You my Help and Guide, governing my life in the ways of peace, and making me worthy to obtain with Your Saints a place at Your right hand, through the prayers and supplications of Your most pure Mother, of Your Angelic Ministers and Powers, and of all Your Saints who from ages have found favor before You. Amen.[13]

PRAYER BEFORE RECEIVING THE BODY AND BLOOD OF CHRIST
FROM ST. ANSELM (1033-1109)
ARCHBISHOP OF CANTERBURY, BENEDICTINE MONK, AND DOCTOR OF THE CHURCH

Lord Jesus Christ, by the Father's plan and by the working of the Holy Ghost of your own free will you died and mercifully redeemed the world from sin and everlasting death.

I adore and venerate you as much as ever I can, though my love is so cold, my devotion so poor.

Thank you for the good gift of this your holy Body and Blood, which I desire to receive, as cleansing from sin, and for a defense against it.

Lord, I acknowledge that I am far from worthy to approach and touch this sacrament; but I trust in that mercy which caused you to lay down your life for sinners that they might be justified, and because you gave yourself willingly as a holy sacrifice to the Father.

A sinner, I presume to receive these gifts so that I may be justified by them.

I beg and pray you, therefore, merciful lover of men, let not that which you have given for the cleansing of sins be unto me the increase of sin, but rather for forgiveness and protection.

Make me, O Lord, so to perceive with lips and

heart and know by faith and by love, that by virtue of this sacrament I may deserve to be planted in the likeness of your death and resurrection, by mortifying the old man, and by renewal of the life of righteousness.

May I be worthy to be incorporated into your body "which is the church," so that I may be your member and you may be my head, and that I may remain in you and you in me.

Then at the Resurrection you will refashion the body of my humiliation according to the body of your glory, as you promised by your apostle, and I shall rejoice in you for ever to your glory, who with the Father and the Holy Spirit lives and reigns for ever. Amen.[14]

PRAYER FROM A 1508 EDITION OF ENGLAND'S SARUM BREVIARY

O glorious Jesus, O meekest Jesus, O most sweet Jesus, I pray you that I may have true confession, contrition, and satisfaction, before I die; and that I may see and receive your holy Body, God and man, Savior of all mankind, Christ Jesus, without sin; and that you will, my Lord God, forgive me all my sins for your glorious wounds; and that I may end my life in the true faith of holy Church, and in perfect love and charity with my fellow Christian as your creature; and I commend my soul into your holy hands, through the glorious help of your blessed Mother of mercy our Lady Saint Mary, and all the holy company of heaven. Amen.

The holy Body of Christ Jesus be my salvation of body and soul. Amen.

The glorious Blood of Christ Jesus bring my soul and body into the everlasting bliss. Amen.

I cry God mercy. I cry God mercy. I cry God mercy. Welcome, my Maker. Welcome, my Redeemer. Welcome, my Saviour. I cry you mercy, with heart contrite of my great unkindness that I have had to you.[15]

"THE SINNER'S BANQUET"
BY ST. AMBROSE (340-397)
ARCHBISHOP OF MILAN AND FATHER OF THE CHURCH

Lord Jesus, you have invited me to your banquet table, though I deserve to be thrown into the dungeon. So I accept your invitation in fear and trembling, encouraged only by your mercy and goodness.

My soul and body are defiled by so many sinful deeds. My tongue and my heart have run wild without restraint, causing misery to others and shame to myself. My soul bleeds with the wounds of wrongdoing, and my body is like a temple of Satan. If I were to come before you as my judge, you could only condemn me to eternal torment, for that is what I deserve.

Yet I come before you, not as a judge, but as a savior. I depend not on your justice, but on your mercy. As you look upon the wretched creature that I am, I ask that your eyes be filled with compassion and forgiveness. And as I sit at your table, I beg you to renew within me a spirit of holiness, that I may be worthy to share your supper.[16]

PRAYER FROM ENGLAND'S
SARUM MISSAL OF 1526
(LARGELY TAKEN FROM A PRAYER OF ST. THOMAS AQUINAS)

Lord, I am not worthy that you should come under my roof, but trusting in your loving kindness I approach your altar; sick I come to the Physician of life, blind to the Light of eternal brightness, poor to the Lord of heaven and earth, naked to the King of glory, a sheep to the Shepherd, a thing formed to Him that formed it, desolate to the kind Comforter, miserable to the pitiful, guilty to the Bestower of pardon, unholy to One that justifies, hardened to the Infuser of grace; imploring the abundance of your boundless mercy that you would

31

vouchsafe to heal my infirmity, to wash my foulness, to enlighten my blindness, to enrich my poverty, to clothe my nakedness, to bring back the wandering, to console the desolate, to reconcile the guilty, to give pardon to the sinner, forgiveness to the wretched, life to the accused, justification to the dead; that I may be deemed worthy to receive you, the Bread of angels, the King of kings, and Lord of lords, with such chastity of body and purity of mind, such contrition of heart and flow of tears, such spiritual happiness and heavenly joy, such fear and trembling, such reverence and honor, such faith and humility, such determination and love, such prayer and thanksgiving, as are becoming and your due, so that I may profitably obtain eternal life, and the remission of all my sins. Amen.[17]

PRAYER OF ST. CAJETAN
(1480-1547)
FOUNDER OF THE THEATINES AND REFORMER

Look down, O Lord, from Thy sanctuary, from Thy dwelling in heaven on high, and behold this sacred Victim which our great High Priest, Thy holy Son our Lord Jesus Christ, offers up to Thee for the sins of His brethren and be appeased despite the multitude of our transgressions. Behold, the voice of the Blood

32

of Jesus, our Brother, cries to Thee from the cross. Give ear, O Lord. Be appeased, O Lord. Hearken and do not delay for Thine own sake, O my God; for Thy Name is invoked upon this city and upon Thy people and deal with us according to Thy mercy. Amen. That Thou wouldst defend, pacify, keep, preserve, and bless this city, we beseech Thee, hear us.[18]

PRAYER BEFORE MASS

O Lord Jesus Christ, how am I to prepare myself to attend that holy sacrifice which you began at your Last Supper and which you consummated on Calvary? That eternal Eucharist begun in sorrow and agony continues, not simply to the end of the world but throughout all eternity. It is the eternal act of obedience and love that you as the head of our whole human race offered to the Trinity, even to yourself in your divinity. These mysteries are completely beyond me. Yet I know they are true because you revealed them. Soon, in the person of a priest, a poor human being, your divine words will be spoken and each of us at this Mass will be lifted beyond this place and be part of the heavenly choirs and the eternal divine liturgy. How dare we think that we, creatures of earth, could participate in such a thing! We believe it because this liturgy began here on earth.

From the very first moment of your existence as a human being, the altar was prepared, the linens were laid on the altar. Throughout your earthly life, you labored in the preaching of the Gospel and in calling the faithful to prayer. Then at the supreme moment of your earthly existence, you offered yourself in total obedience and sacrifice to the Father for all the world. Your glorious Resurrection and Ascension point beyond the cross and beyond the tomb, and remind us that this Eucharist is not only a memorial but an everlasting participation in your divine and heavenly worship as priest of the new creation.

O Lord, give me your Holy Spirit that my heart may be lifted up in this Mass, that I may be in one of the choirs that join with you, that I may take my place prayerfully and in reverent attention with the billions of saints, with the great choirs of angels, with the army of holy souls on their pilgrimage and with all the devout and struggling Christians in the world. Let this Mass be the beginning of a new moment in my life, one step closer to you. May I be encouraged by this sacred meal to know that you will go with me in the wilderness of life, that you will sustain me so that I may, in fact, not only pray as one of those united to you, but that I may live and act so that it may indeed be true that I live, no longer I, but you live in me. Amen.

— BJG

THANKSGIVING AFTER HOLY COMMUNION

FROM A LETTER OF THE VENERABLE PADRE PIO OF PIETRELCINA
(1887-1968)
CAPUCHIN FRIAR AND STIGMATIST

When Mass was over I remained with Jesus in thanksgiving. Oh, how sweet was the colloquy with paradise that morning! It was such that, although I want to tell you all about it, I cannot. There were things which cannot be translated into human language without losing their deep and heavenly meaning. The heart of Jesus and my own — allow me to use the expression — were fused. No longer were two hearts beating but only one. My own heart had disappeared, as a drop of water is lost in the ocean. Jesus was its paradise, its king. My joy was so intense and deep that I could bear no more and tears of happiness poured down my cheeks.[19]

From the Autobiography of
St. Teresa of Ávila
(1515-1582)
*Founder of the Discalced Carmelites
and Doctor of the Church*

O Wealth of the poor, how admirably You know how to sustain souls! And without their seeing such great wealth, You show it to them little by little. When I behold majesty as extraordinary as this concealed in something as small as the host, it happens afterward that I marvel at wisdom so wonderful, and I fail to know how the Lord gives me the courage or strength to approach Him.[20]

Prayer of St. Augustine
(354-430)
Bishop of Hippo and Father of the Church

Jesus, for your namesake,
do that which your name proclaims.
Jesus, pardon the pride that pains you
and look upon the unhappy one
that calls upon your tender name —
name of comfort, name of delight,
and to sinners name of blessed hope.

For what does your name mean, Jesus, but
    Savior?
Therefore, for your name's sake
be to me, Jesus, a merciful Savior.[21]

"TO CHRIST THE LORD"
BY ST. SYMEON (TENTH CENTURY)
*HAGIOGRAPHER AND SECRETARY OF STATE TO THE BYZANTINE
EMPEROR ROMANOS II*

You, my Creator, Who for Meat
freely have given me Your Flesh,
Who are a fire consuming the unworthy:
O consume me not!
rather, enter into my members ...
into my very heart and veins!

Burn up, like thorns, all my sins!
Purge my soul,
and sanctify my imagination! ...
Shine into all the darks of my five senses!
Fasten me wholly in the fear of You!

Guard me! shield, shelter me evermore
from every word and deed which stains the soul.
Cleanse, wash, adorn me, set me right!

Give me understanding and enlighten me.
Prove me the habitation of Your Spirit only,
nowise the dwelling place of sin.
Praying and interceding for me are all the saints,
whom now I set before You,
the princes of the bodiless orders,
Your forerunners, the wise Apostles, and withal
Your pure, Your spotless Mother:
accept their prayers, my Christ, in Your
  Compassion!
Of Your servant make a child of Light![22]

PRAYER FOR HOLY SATURDAY
(THIRD OR FOURTH CENTURY)

Today we have seen
  our Lord Jesus Christ on the altar.
Today we have gained possession
  of the burning coal in whose shadow
  the cherubim sing.
Today we have heard
  a voice say, sweet and strong:

This body burns the thorns of sin.
This body gives light to the souls
  of all believers.

This body the woman touched
    that had the flux of blood,
    and gone was her bitter anguish …
See, children, what a body
    we have eaten, see what blood
    we have drunk, what a covenant
    we have made with our God.
O to be proof against shame
    on the day of requital.

Who can sufficiently praise
    the mystery of your grace?
We have been enabled
    to take our share of the gift;
    may we keep it safe to the end,
    that so we may come to hear
    the blessed voice,
    the sweet, the holy, saying:
Come, you that have received
    a blessing from my Father;
    take possession of the kingdom
    that awaits you.[23]

PRAYER OF ST. THOMAS AQUINAS
(CA. 1225-1274)
DOMINICAN FRIAR AND DOCTOR OF THE CHURCH

O Most Sweet Jesus, My Lord and Master, O that the force of your love, subtler than fire, and sweeter than honey, would engulf my soul in an abyss, drawing it from all inordinate affections to things beneath Heaven; that I might die with love of you, since out of love you did vouchsafe to die on the Cross for me![24]

ANIMA CHRISTI
ANONYMOUS (FOURTEENTH CENTURY)
TRANSLATION BY CARDINAL NEWMAN

Soul of Christ, be my sanctification;
Body of Christ, be my salvation;
Blood of Christ, all fill my veins;
Water of Christ's side, wash out my stains;
Passion of Christ, my comfort be;
O good Jesu, listen to me;
In Thy wounds I fain would hide,
Ne'er to be parted from Thy side;
Guard me should the foe assail me;
Call me when my life shall fail me;
Bid me come to Thee above,

With Thy saints to sing Thy love,
World without end. Amen.[25]

"RADIATING CHRIST"
A PRAYER ADAPTED FROM THE WRITINGS OF
THE VENERABLE JOHN HENRY NEWMAN
BY THE MISSIONARIES OF CHARITY

Dear Jesus, help us to spread your fragrance everywhere we go. / Flood our souls with your spirit and life. / Penetrate and possess our whole being, / so utterly, / that our lives may only be a radiance of yours. / Shine through us, / and be so in us, / that every soul we come in contact with / may feel your presence in our soul. / Let them look up and see no longer us /but only Jesus! / Stay with us, / and then we shall begin to shine as you shine; / so to shine as to be a light to others; / the light, O Jesus, will be all from you, / none of it will be ours; / it will be you, shining on others through us. / Let us thus praise you in the way you love best / by shining on those around us. / Let us preach you without preaching, / not by words but by our example, / by the catching force, / the sympathetic influence of what we do, / the evident fullness of the love our hearts bear to you. Amen.[26]

AVE VERUM
(FOURTEENTH CENTURY)

Hail, true Body, truly born
Of the Virgin Mary mild,
Truly offered, racked and torn,
On the Cross, for man defiled,
From whose love-pierced, sacred side
Flowed Thy true Blood's saving tide:
Be a foretaste sweet to me
In my death's great agony,
O Thou loving, gentle One,
Sweetest Jesus, Mary's Son.[27]

PRAYER FROM AN ELEVENTH-CENTURY MANUSCRIPT OF WINCHESTER

Jesus, our Lord and God, who are to us the way, the truth, and the life, to You do we pray that You would make us partakers of eternal happiness. You have brought down from heaven true life into the world. We acknowledge You as that Bread of Life which strengthens the heart of man, for whosoever shall come to You shall never hunger, whosoever shall believe in You shall not thirst for ever. Your flesh, O God Omnipotent, is verily food, and Your blood,

O Jesus, is drink to Your faithful children. By this mystery You have redeemed us from death, O Lord, in order that we might live in You with constancy and heedfulness. Deign, therefore, we beseech You, to let us partake in this holy mystery to the praise of Your name. It is Your commandment, O Christ, that we love one another; helped by this Your gift, we are enabled to fulfill this law. Thus is Your charity poured forth into our souls, till at length love of others so springs up in our hearts that no wicked hatred, nor deep envy, nor strong malice can remain in them. For the sake of Your holy Body, pardon the faults we have committed through the frailty of our flesh. O Christ, who alone are all pure, by the power of Your grace wash away every spot from our minds, and every stain from our souls. O God, who are the true peace, keep our souls undisturbed, we beseech You, and our minds at rest in You; for where there is peace You Yourself are present, and where You are all that is there is Yours. Come therefore, O Lord, and take possession of us for ever, and let us be the true temples of Your Holy Spirit.[28]

PRAYER OF
ST. CATHERINE OF SIENA (1347-1380)
THIRD ORDER DOMINICAN AND DOCTOR OF THE CHURCH

O boundless charity!
Just as you gave us yourself,
wholly God and wholly man,
so you left us all of yourself as food
so that while we are pilgrims in this life
we might not collapse in our weariness
but be strengthened by you, heavenly food.
O mercenary people!
And what has your God left you?
He has left you himself,
wholly God and wholly man,
hidden under the whiteness of this bread.
O fire of love!
Was it not enough to gift us
with creation in your image and likeness,
and to create us anew to grace in your Son's blood,
without giving us yourself as food,
the whole of divine being,
the whole of God?
What drove you?
Nothing but your charity,
mad with love as you are![29]

PRAYER ATTRIBUTED TO ST. JOHN CHYSOSTOM

FROM THE ARMENIAN LITURGY

I give thanks unto You, I magnify and glorify You, O Lord my God, inasmuch as this day You have vouchsafed me, unworthy as I am, to be partaker of the divine and awful mysteries of Your most pure Body and Blood.

Having this for my defense, I beseech You that every day of my life You would keep me in Your holiness; so that by commemorating Your goodness and Your bounties I may live with You: for You, O my Lord and God, did suffer, die, and rise again for our sakes. Let not the enemy approach to hurt my soul which has been sealed with the sign of Your most precious Blood, and cleanse me, O Lord God, from all my mortal sins, for You alone are without sin.

O Lord God, protect my life from all misfortunes, drive away my enemies, and all who would do me evil; strengthen and establish my feet, my thoughts, my tongue, and all the ways of my body; be You always with me according to Your most sure promise: He that eats My Flesh and drinks My Blood dwells in Me and I in him. You have said this, O Lover of mankind; confirm these blessed words, Your inviolable declarations, for You, O God, are merciful, bountiful, and the Lover of mankind; You give every good thing, and to You belongs glory, with the Father and the Holy Spirit now and for ever, world without end. Amen.[30]

PRAYER OF ST. BONAVENTURE
(1215-1274)
MINISTER GENERAL OF THE FRANCISCAN ORDER, CARDINAL-BISHOP OF ALBANO, AND DOCTOR OF THE CHURCH

Pierce my inmost soul, O most sweet Jesus, with the most sweet and beneficial wound of Your love and with true, sincere, apostolic and most holy charity, so that my soul may suffer and wither with longing because of that same love and the desire for You; may it long for You only and consume itself by that desire for Your dwelling, and may it aspire to be free from the bonds of the flesh and to remain always with You.

Grant that my soul may hunger for You, the Bread of the Angels, the Refreshment of holy souls, our daily Bread, that gives us strength and contains in Itself every sweetness, every delight and every pleasing taste. May my heart yearn only to feed upon You, whom the angels desire to look upon, and may my soul be filled with the sweetness of Your savor. May it ever thirst after You, the Fountain of life, the Fountain of wisdom and knowledge, the Fountain of eternal light, the Torrent of every delight, the Wealth

46

of the house of God.

May I always desire ardently for You, search for You, find You, sigh for You, meditate upon You, speak of You, and do all things for the glory of Your Name, with humility and prudence, with love and pleasure, with ease and affection, with perseverance unto the end.

Be always, You alone, my hope, my whole confidence, my wealth, my delight, my joy, my happiness, my rest and my serenity. Be my peace, my sweetness, my perfume, my food, my nourishment, my refuge, my possession. Finally, be my treasure, in whom my mind and my heart may remain fixed, firm and immovably rooted forever. Amen.[31]

"PRAYER OF THANKSGIVING"
FROM THE ARMENIAN LITURGY

We render thanks unto You, O Christ our God, who of Your goodness have bestowed upon us the Food for the sanctification of our lives; keep us through It holy and without blame under Your divine protection; feed us in the pastures of Your holy and good pleasure, that, being strengthened against all snares of the devil, we may be deemed worthy to hear Your holy voice, and follow You, the one victorious and true Shepherd, and to receive from You that place which has been prepared for us in the Kingdom of Heaven. For You, O our God and Lord and Savior Jesus Christ, are blessed with the Father and the Holy Spirit now, and for ever, and world without end. Amen.[32]

AFTER HOLY COMMUNION

O Lord, I have been to your sacred banquet. I have been fed with the bread of angels made the bread of mortal human beings. It is beyond me! Into my own being in the most intimate way you, the Savior of the world, have come to me. How much joy filled the apostles when you came to the upper room after the Resurrection. With what joy did they see you before your glorious Ascension. With what gratitude did Paul realize that he had met you on the road to Damascus. How many times in the history of your Church have the great saints encountered you in some visible way so that they might be strengthened in their arduous task.

Although you have come to me in no startling way, you nonetheless have come to me who am a poor, weak, and sinful person. You have cared about me. You have taken me by the hand and led me. You have grasped me around the shoulders and kept me from falling. You have been there for me when I have failed.

O Lord, let me accept all that this day may bring as coming from you. May my life be joined with your sacrifice for patience, obedience, and love. As I leave this Sacred Banquet filled with the grace of this Holy Communion, may I bring you to others by kindness, by generosity, by forgiveness, by patience, by love. Help me to break out of the prison of my own self-concern, of what I think is important. Give me the grace to be you to others and to find you in them. This is the true meaning of Holy Communion. This is the bond that links us with all believers and through your charity to all the children of God. Be with me, O Lord, throughout the day as you have come to me in this Holy Communion. And if you are with me and your Holy Spirit reminds me of this, then I shall do what you have done. I shall try to do his will always by the grace of the Holy Spirit. Amen.

— BJG

THE VISIT TO CHRIST IN THE EUCHARIST: PRAYERS FOR A HOLY HOUR AND EXPOSITION

For at least eight hundred years — and perhaps up to fourteen hundred years — devout people have kept vigil with Christ in the Eucharist. The Sacrament focuses our attention and gives assurance to our faith that He is with us. Devoutly to approach Christ hidden in this mystery is to become renewed in the Christian life. To show both exterior and interior signs of reverence is to be lifted beyond the commonplace, to remember spiritual realities as Saint Paul advises. Silence, reverence, gratitude, loving devotion can flood the soul if one is blessed to do this for an hour. Certainly it fulfills the invitation of Christ, "... could you not watch with me one hour?" (Mt 26:40).

To increase our devotion the mystical sign, the consecrated Host, is exposed in a monstrance. The Host mysteriously fulfills Christ's promise of His presence — "This is my Body ... this is my Blood." The custom of exposing the Sacrament as we do now began in the thirteenth century and is an especially powerful invitation to loving meditation and con- templation. It is the center of life for many cloistered

51

communities of contemplative nuns; it can be the same for the devout person blessed to have exposition in a parish church or chapel.

FROM A TALK OF THE VENERABLE FATHER SOLANUS CASEY
(1870-1957)
PORTER OF ST. BONAVENTURE'S MONASTERY, DETROIT

What does it matter where we go? Wherever we go, won't we be serving God there? And wherever we go, won't we have Our Lord in the Blessed Sacrament with us? Isn't that enough to make us happy?[33]

FROM THE WRITINGS OF ST. PETER JULIAN EYMARD
(1811-1868)
FOUNDER OF THE
BLESSED SACRAMENT FATHERS AND BROTHERS

Oh! Yes, Lord Jesus, come and reign! Let my body be Your temple, my heart Your throne, my will Your devoted servant; let me be Yours forever, living only of You and for You![34]

"A SHORT VISIT TO THE BLESSED SACRAMENT"

VENERABLE JOHN HENRY NEWMAN

I place myself in the presence of Him, in whose Incarnate Presence I am before I place myself there.

I adore Thee, O my Saviour, present here as God and man, in soul and body, in true flesh and blood.

I acknowledge and confess that I kneel before that Sacred Humanity, which was conceived in Mary's womb, and lay in Mary's bosom; which grew up to man's estate, and by the Sea of Galilee called the Twelve, wrought miracles, and spoke words of wisdom and peace; which in due season hung on the cross, lay in the tomb, rose from the dead, and now reigns in heaven.

I praise, and bless, and give myself wholly to Him, who is the true Bread of my soul, and my everlasting joy.[35]

"ACT WHEN VISITING THE MOST HOLY SACRAMENT" ST. ALPHONSUS LIGUORI (1696-1787)

FOUNDER OF THE REDEMPTORISTS AND DOCTOR OF THE CHURCH

My Lord Jesus Christ, who, for the love You bear to mankind, do remain night and day in this Sacrament, full of pity and love, awaiting, calling, and receiving all who come to visit You; I believe that You are present in the Sacrament of the Altar; I adore You from the depths of my own nothingness; I thank You for the many graces You have given me, and especially for having given me Yourself in this Sacrament; for having given me Mary Your Mother as my advocate, and for having called me to visit You in this church ... My Jesus, I love You with my whole heart. I am sorry that I have formerly so often offended Your infinite goodness. With the help of Your grace, I resolve to displease You no more; and, unworthy as I am, I now consecrate myself wholly to You; I renounce and give to You my will, my affections, my desires, and all that is mine. Henceforward do with me, and all that belongs to me, whatsoever You please. I ask for nothing but You and Your holy love, final perseverance, and a perfect fulfillment of Your will.[36]

"LIVING ON LOVE"
ST. THÉRÈSE OF LISIEUX (1873-1897)
(COMPOSED DURING FORTY HOURS DEVOTION, 1895)

On the evening of Love, speaking without parable, / Jesus said: "If anyone wishes to love me / All his life, let him keep my Word. / My Father and I will come to visit him. / And we will make his heart our dwelling. / Coming to him, we shall love him always. / We want him to remain, filled with peace, / In our Love! ..."

Living on Love is living on your life, / Glorious King, delight of the elect. / You live for me, hidden in a host. / I want to hide myself for you, O Jesus! / Lovers must have solitude, / A heart-to-heart lasting night and day. Just one glance of yours makes my beatitude. / I live on Love! ...

Living on Love is not setting up one's tent/ At the top of Tabor. / It's climbing Calvary with Jesus. /

It's looking at the Cross as a treasure! ... / In Heaven I'm to live on joy. / Then trials will have fled forever, / But in exile, in suffering I want To live on Love.

Living on Love is imitating Mary, / Bathing your divine feet that she kisses, transported. / With tears, with precious perfume, / She dries them with her long hair.... / Then standing up, she shatters the vase, And in turn she anoints your Sweet Face. / As for me, the perfume with which I anoint your Face / Is my Love! ...[37]

PRAYER TO JESUS IN THE BLESSED SACRAMENT
POPE JOHN XXIII (1958-1963)

O Jesus, King of all peoples and all ages, accept the acts of adoration and praise which we, your brothers by adoption, humbly offer you.

You are the "living Bread which comes down from heaven and gives life to the world" (Jn 6:33), Supreme Priest and Victim. On the Cross you offered yourself to the Eternal Father as a bloody sacrifice of expiation, for the redemption of the human race, and now you offer yourself daily upon our altars by the hands of your ministers, in order to establish in every heart your "reign of truth and life, of holiness and grace, of justice, love and peace" (Preface of the Mass of Christ the King).

O King of glory, may your kingdom come! Reign from your "throne of grace" (Heb 4: 14), in the hearts of children, so that they may guard untainted the white lily of baptismal innocence. Reign in the hearts of the young, that they may grow up healthy and pure, obedient to the commands of those who represent you in their families and schools and in the Church. Reign in our homes, so that parents and children may live in peace in obedience to your holy law. Reign in our land, so that all citizens, in the harmonious order of the various social groups, may feel themselves children of the same heavenly Father, called to co-operate for the common good of this world, happy to belong to the one Mystical Body, of which your Sacrament is at once the symbol and the everlasting source.

Finally, reign, O King of kings and "Lord of lords," (Deut 10:17) over all the nations of the earth, and enlighten all their rulers in order that, inspired by your example, they may make "plans for welfare and not for evil" (Jer 29:11).

O Jesus, present in the Sacrament of the Altar, teach all the nations to serve you with willing hearts, knowing that "to serve God is to reign." May your Sacrament, O Jesus, be light to the mind, strength to the will, joy to the heart. May it be the support of the weak, the comfort of the suffering, the wayfaring bread of salvation for the dying, and for all the "pledge of future glory." Amen.[38]

PRAYER IN BLESSED SACRAMENT CHAPEL, SAINT PETER'S BASILICA, INAUGURATING PERPETUAL ADORATION, 1981

POPE JOHN PAUL II

"Lord, stay with us."

These words were spoken for the first time by the disciples of Emmaus. Subsequently in the course of the centuries they have been spoken, infinite times, by the lips of so many of your disciples and confessors, O Christ.

... I speak the same words today.

I speak them to invite you, Christ, in your Eucharistic presence, to accept the daily adoration continuing through the entire day, in this temple, in this basilica, in this chapel.

Stay with us today and stay, from now on, every day, according to the desire of my heart....

Stay! That we may meet you in prayer of adoration and thanksgiving, in prayer of expiation and petition, to which all those who visit this basilica are invited.

Stay! You who are at one and the same time veiled in the Eucharistic mystery of faith and also revealed under the species of bread and wine, which you have assumed in this Sacrament.

Stay! That your presence in this temple may incessantly be reconfirmed, and all those who enter here may become aware that it is your house, "the dwelling of God with men" (Rev 21:3) and, visiting this basilica, may find in it the very source "of life and holiness that gushes from your Eucharistic Heart." ...

Every day and every hour we wish to adore you, stripped under the species of bread and wine, to renew hopes of the "call to glory" (cf. 1 Pet 5:10), the beginning of which you constituted with your glorified body "at the Father's right hand."[39]

"PRAYER BEFORE LEAVING FOR APOSTOLATE"
(MISSIONARIES OF CHARITY OF MOTHER TERESA)

Dear Lord, the Great Healer, I kneel before You, since every perfect gift must come from You. I pray, give skill to my hands, clear vision to my mind, kindness and meekness to my heart. Give me singleness of purpose, strength to lift up a part of the burden of my suffering fellow men, and a true realization of the privilege that is mine. Take from my heart all guile and worldliness that with the simple faith of a child, I may rely on You. Amen.[40]

PRAYER OF ST. COLUMBANUS (+615)
IRISH MONK AND MISSIONARY

Lord, I pray that you may be a lamp for me in the darkness. Touch my soul and kindle a fire within it, that it may burn brightly and give light to my life. Thus my body may truly become your temple, lit by your perpetual flame burning on the altar of my heart. And may the light within me shine on my brethren that it may drive away the darkness of ignorance and sin from them also. Thus together let us be lights to the world, manifesting the bright beauty of your gospel to all around us.[41]

PRAYER OF ST. JOHN EUDES (1601-1680)
FOUNDER OF THE EUDISTS

O Jesus my Lord, I cast myself down and efface myself at Your feet; I surrender myself to the might of Your divine spirit and Your holy love, in their immense power and greatness; I adore, glorify and love You in Yourself and in all the mysteries and phases of Your life. I adore You in Your temporal life on earth for thirty-four years. I adore You in the first moment of that life, in Your holy Childhood, in Your hidden life of labor, in Your public ministry among men, both when You did live and walk on earth for all to see, and now that You are still among us in the Blessed Eucharist. I adore You in all Your sufferings, interior and exterior, and in the last moment of Your passible life. I adore You in Your life of glory and bliss in heaven ever since the Ascension. I adore You in Your life in the most Blessed Virgin and in all the angels and saints, whether in heaven or on earth. And, in general, I adore, love and glorify You in all the other mysteries and wonders that are embraced in the measureless expanse of Your life, divine, temporal and glorified. I bless You and give You infinite thanks for all the glory You did ever and ever shall render to the Father in all the phases of Your life.

I offer You all the love and honor You ever did or shall receive forever, in all Your mysteries and states, from all the angels and all the saints, begging them most humbly to love and glorify You, for me, in every way possible and fitting to Your glory.[42]

PRAYER OF ST. THOMAS MORE (1478-1535)
LORD CHANCELLOR OF ENGLAND AND MARTYR

Give me, good Lord, a full faith, a firm hope,
and a fervent charity, a love to you, good Lord,
incomparably above the love to myself,
and that I love nothing to your displeasure,
but everything in an order to you ...
Take from me, good Lord, this lukewarm fashion,
or rather my cold manner of meditation,
and this dullness in praying unto you.
And give me warmth, delight and quickness
in thinking upon you; and give me your grace
to long for your holy sacraments,
and specially to rejoice in the presence
of your very blessed body (sweet Savior Christ,
in the holy sacrament of the altar),
and duly to thank you for your gracious
visitation therewith, and at that high memorial,
with tender compassion, to remember and
consider your most bitter passion.[43]

PRAYER FROM AN ARGENTINE DEVOTIONAL BOOK, 1985, FOR THE EUCHARISTIC VIGIL OF HOLY THURSDAY

(BUT SUITABLE FOR OTHER TIMES AS WELL)

Merciful Savior, this holy night we remember your testament of love and the painful agony of your soul, sad unto death.

We wish to accompany you spiritually into the Garden of Olives, responding to your repeated invitation to watch and pray at least an hour with you.

We know that upon your shoulders weighed our sins as well and that in the bitter chalice were also our faults and our infidelity.

We offer you, therefore, this hour of adoration as a proper act of reparation and love.

Purify, Jesus, our souls, free us from mortifying tepidity and help us not to fall into temptation.

In those dark moments of affliction and of discouragement, bring about that we may imitate you who, in prolonged prayer, find the strength to follow fully the will of the Father and to face with courage your Passion.

Suffering Jesus, we thank you and we love you. Bring about that we may live and die for you.[44]

A HOLY HOUR PRAYER

O Lord, thank you for this hour of Eucharistic devotion. It comes as a time of peace, recollection, and healing. How privileged I am to spend an hour with you! It makes me feel like the apostles and the disciples who were able to speak quietly with you along the road, perhaps sitting under a tree in the evening.

What am I to say to you? You know everything about me. You know all my needs, all my failings — and even my good intentions. In this hour I adore you as the infinite and Holy One of God. You and the Father are one and you have promised that we will be one in you. I give you thanks for all the blessings of my life which I so seldom think of. I thank you for life itself, material and spiritual.

I ask your forgiveness and healing for all my short-comings and sins; all the times that unthinkingly I have failed you and fallen short of the grace that you gave me. And finally I place before you confidently everyone that I care about, every concern that I have, every need of my life. I promise to trust you no matter what happens to me. You will bring good out of even the worst of it. I do not ask you to change what is to be. Rather, in whatever there is to be, let me find your will, your holiness, and your opportunity for me to grow. I will try to say, "I know that you are with me." Finally, I redirect my life, my desires, my hopes, to you, not only for myself but for all whom I care about and for the whole world. May your kingdom come. May your Holy Spirit be with us. Send him constantly to us as you promised you would at the Last Supper.

As I look it this mysterious sign, the white host, my eyes tell me nothing of who is there, but faith affirms in my heart that you, my Lord and God, are there. I thank you for this precious gift of faith. Amen.

— BJG

A VISIT AT THE START OF THE DAY

Jesus, the day begins, a new opportunity, a clean slate, new work to be done. The day is not yet marred by my weakness and distraction, by my impatience and self-love. It is fresh and new, your gift to me. I am so grateful this morning to be in your Eucharistic presence. It is like your apostles waking up to find themselves along the road in Galilee, perhaps having slept near you under a tree or in the shelter of an old building. I look at the tabernacle, toward its glowing candles. Your shining presence there invites me to a new day, to start afresh. Your love in giving me your Eucharistic presence — which is just as real as your presence at Nazareth — fills me with great confidence as the day begins. I ask you to come with me when I leave this church, when duty and responsibility call me forth to begin the day. I ask you to be the unseen presence in all that I do. I am well aware that I will not do it well, that there will be many shortcomings, perhaps even sins. But you put up with your apostles and disciples. Even when you called them to task you also forgave them. Come with me and call me back on the path by your providence. But especially be with me that I may show to others a small reflection of the wealth that you give us by being with us at the beginning of every day until the end of the world. Amen.

— BJG

A VISIT DURING THE DAY

O Lord Jesus Christ, this day is very busy. I am distracted and pulled in many directions. There are concerns, worries, even fears. I am troubled about duties, failures, things to do that are beyond me. I come to your presence from the din of life, the noise of the street, from the pleas and demands of others. And you are here. For a moment I am with you by the Sea of Galilee, on the Mount of Beatitudes, looking at the serene water and the green hills. You say, "Come to me, all you who are weary and find life burdensome, and I will refresh you." Your presence in the Eucharist reassures me that this is true.

You will be with me when I leave the chapel, but then I will not know where to turn my eyes or how to lift my heart. But here I know. Your signature is on all of creation, on the world about us. But it is often impossible for me to read. But here in the silence I am with you. You invited your disciples, "Come apart and rest a while." I am here. Give me, in these few moments, the fullness of your Spirit that I may know that you are with me, that I may go back to the tasks of life assured that you are beside me. Then I shall be at peace to do your will. Amen.

— BJG

A Visit at the End of the Day

O Divine Master, I come before you as the evening shadows gather and the day ends. This day is like so many others — your presence, your gifts, the opportunities of your grace have been marred by my failings, by my self-centeredness. I have failed others today. I have responded in no way in proportion to the immense graces that you have given me. But here you are waiting for me in your silent presence! It is both a motive for contrition and a motive for hope. You wait for me in silence. You wait for each one. Even notorious sinners can come and kneel before your tabernacle.

Jesus, you are the father of the poor. You are the one who forgives the sinner. I come and place my day before you and again I know I shall be healed. I am absolutely sure of your forgiving love because you have chosen to be with us, every morning, every day, every evening until, finally, the last evening of this world comes and we pass from this place of change and time to the endless day of your divine presence. I place before you all who will die this day. Send your Holy Spirit upon them all.

I place before you all of my family and my friends. Guide and enlighten each of us. I entrust to you all who have need of conversion.

Take my tomorrow into your wounded hands and I will be able to rest securely. Amen.

— BJG

THE EUCHARISTIC PROCESSION

The custom of carrying the Eucharist in a solemn procession allowing public veneration to Christ the King existed by the eleventh century when it was introduced at Canterbury Cathedral in the Palm Sunday procession. It became a very powerful expression of Christian piety in many countries. Peasant and pope, beggar and prince, poor sinner and nun, soldier and artisan, old and young enjoyed the opportunity for all to kneel together before the King of Kings, who would come at the end of the ages. The great feast of the Eucharist, Corpus Christi, called forth music, art, and every talent to the worship of Jesus Christ whose second coming we await. Literally, in this Sacrament we proclaim the death and resurrection of the Lord until He comes. Even if you cannot enjoy a Eucharistic procession, the following hymns are beautiful and instructive.

ADORO TE DEVOTE
BY ST. THOMAS AQUINAS

Hidden God, devoutly I adore thee,
Truly present underneath these veils:
All my heart subdues itself before thee,
Since it all before thee faints and fails.
Not to sight, or taste, or touch be credit,
Hearing only do we trust secure;
I believe, for God the Son hath said it -
Word of Truth that ever shall endure.
On the Cross was veiled thy Godhead's splendor,
Here thy Manhood lieth hidden too;
Unto both alike my faith I render,
And, as sued the contrite thief, I sue.
Though I look not on thy wounds, with Thomas,
Thee, my Lord, and thee, my God I call:
Make me more and more believe thy promise,
Hope in thee, and love thee over all.
O Memorial of my Savior dying,
Living Bread, that givest life to man;
May my soul, its life from thee supplying,
Taste thy sweetness, as on earth it can.
Deign, O Jesus, Pelican of heaven,
Me, a sinner, in thy blood to lave,
To a single drop of which is given
All the world from all its sin to save.
Contemplating, Lord, thy hidden presence,

Grant me what I thirst for and implore,
In the revelation of thine essence
To behold thy glory evermore. Amen.[45]

PANGE LINGUA GLORIOSI
BY ST. THOMAS AQUINAS

Sing, my tongue, the Savior's glory,
Of His Flesh the mystery sing;
Of the Blood, all price exceeding,
Shed by our immortal King,
Destined, for the world's redemption,

From a noble womb to spring.
On the night of that Last Supper
Seated with His chosen band,
He, the Paschal victim eating,
First fulfills the Law's command:
Then as Food to all His brethren
Gives Himself with His own hand.

Down in adoration falling,
Lo! the sacred Host we hail;
Lo! o'er ancient forms departing,
Newer rites of grace prevail;
Faith for all defects supplying,
Where the feeble senses fail.[46]

71

LAUDA SION
BY ST. THOMAS AQUINAS

Praise, O Sion, your Redeemer.
Praise your Prince and Shepherd
With canticle and hymn.

Dare to praise Him as you can,
For He is greater than all praise.
Our brightest praises are but dim.

This truth to Christians is proclaimed:
That to flesh, bread is transformed,
And transformed to blood is wine.

Good Shepherd, Bread of Truth,
Lord Jesus, show Your clemency.
May You feed us, may You guard us,
May You let us see good things
In our homeland eternally.

You Who know and do all things
Feed us, though still captive here.
Make us fellow-citizens,
Co-heirs, and friends of all the saints
In that City bright and clear.
Amen.[47]

PRAYER OF POPE JOHN PAUL II
FOR A EUCHARISTIC PROCESSION

... Lord Jesus, who in the Eucharist make your dwelling among us and become our travelling companion, sustain our *Christian communities* so that they may be ever more open to listening and accepting your Word. May they draw from the Eucharist a renewed commitment to spreading in society, by the proclamation of your Gospel, the signs and deeds of an attentive and active charity.

Lord Jesus, in your Eucharist make *Christian spouses* the "signs" of your nuptial love among us; make *families* communities of people who, living in dialogue with God and each other, do not fear life and become responsible for sowing the seeds of priestly, religious and missionary vocations.

Lord Jesus, from your altar illuminate *this* city with light and grace, so that it may reject the seduction of a materialistic conception of life, and defeat the selfishness that threatens it, the injustices that upset it, and the divisions with which it is afflicted.

Lord Jesus: give us your joy, give us your peace. Stay with us, Lord!

You alone have the words of eternal life![48]

THE VISIT FROM AFAR

Sometimes one cannot enter a church to adore the Eucharistic presence. Perhaps one can only see the steeple as did the shepherd Saint Paschal Baylon when he prayed in the fields. Perhaps one is ill at home and can only attend to the Eucharist on television, recalling an event in the life of Saint Clare of Assisi, who told of seeing the Christmas liturgy when she was too ill to attend. In our day a fine young man, Eugene Hamilton, ordained a priest in the hour of death, spoke of his hospital room as a chapel. He could spend hours in prayer before the Eucharist visible on the in-house television of Good Samaritan Hospital in Suffern, New York. Perhaps one must pray without the Sacrament and simply honor the Eucharistic presence of Christ from afar, as Bishop James Walsh the missionary did when he was imprisoned in China. Distances of time or place are no obstacle to God, nor should they be for the faithful soul. Every Mass, every visit should continue throughout the day, so that throughout all of life the Christian soul may respond to Christ's promise: "Yes, Jesus, my Savior, I also will be with you to the end of the ages."

AWAY FROM THE EUCHARISTIC PRESENCE

O Lord, I now have a few minutes here away from the tabernacle. You are not here in your sacramental presence. I know you are present everywhere. Yet I wish I now had the reassurance of your presence in the Eucharist. You are here now as you are everywhere because you are the Word of God through whom all things are made. You are present in the most remote places. You are present in the most remote parts of the earth, in the depths of the sea, in the mysterious planets and the most distant stars. If I meet only one other Christian and we speak of you or to you, you are there.

But I need to be near you as you were here on earth in your humanity as well as your divinity. I know that your sacramental presence is not far from me … in a church in that little town I see from the airplane window or in the locked church whose steeple I see from the highway. I'm consoled that you are there. The world is made sacred by your presence. May I have the grace to yearn to be with you so that when I come to your sacramental presence I may be all the more reverent, thankful, and filled with adoration. I know that I will be with you soon — and that consoles me. Meanwhile, send your Holy Spirit upon me and all those dear to me that we will be strengthened. In the storms of life, keep all of us at peace in the knowledge that you are with us and that you await our coming at the end of our journey. Amen.

— BJG

SCRIPTURE FOR EUCHARISTIC MEDITATION

Then I will go to the altar of God,
to God my exceeding joy....

[Ps 43:4]

... Jesus took bread, and blessed, and broke it, and gave it to the disciples and said, "Take, eat; this is my body." And he took a cup, and when he had given thanks he gave it to them, saying, "Drink of it, all of you; for this is my blood of the covenant, which is poured out for many for the forgiveness of sins...."

[Mt 26:26-28]

For from the rising of the sun to its setting my name is great among the nations, and in every place incense is offered to my name, and a pure offering....

[Mal 1:11]

For I received from the Lord what I also delivered to you, that the Lord Jesus on the night when he was betrayed took bread, and when he had given thanks, he broke it, and said, "This is my body which is for you. Do this in remembrance of me." In the same way also the cup, after supper, saying, "This cup is the new covenant in my blood. Do this, as often as you drink it, in remembrance of me." For as often as you eat this bread and drink the cup, you proclaim the Lord's death until he comes.

[1 Cor 11:23-26]

The steadfast love of the LORD never ceases,
    his mercies never come to an end;
they are new every morning....

[Lam 3:22-23]

"I am the living bread which came down from heaven; if any one eats of this bread, he will live for ever; and the bread which I shall give for the life of the world is my flesh."

[Jn 6:51]

As a hart longs for flowing streams,
so longs my soul
    for thee, O God.
My soul thirsts for God,
    for the living God.

[Ps 42:1-2]

My Lord and my God!

[Jn 20:28]

"Truly, truly, I say to you, unless you eat the flesh of the Son of man and drink his blood, you have no life in you; he who eats my flesh and drinks my blood has eternal life, and I will raise him up at the last day. For my flesh is food indeed, and my blood is drink indeed. He who eats my flesh and drinks my blood abides in me, and I in him."

[Jn 6:53-56]

And walk in love, as Christ loved us and gave himself up for us, a fragrant offering and sacrifice to God.
[Eph 5:2]

"I will not leave you desolate; I will come to you."
[Jn 14:18]

"... Remain here, and watch with me."
[Mt 26:38]

"Could you not watch one hour?"
[Mk 14:37]

"If any one serves me, he must follow me; and where I am, there shall my servant be also...."
[Jn 12:26]

"… Put off your shoes from your feet, for the place on which you are standing is holy ground."

[Ex 3:5]

"And you shall put the mercy seat on the top of the ark; and in the ark you shall put the testimony that I shall give you. There I will meet with you, and from above the mercy seat, from between the two cherubim that are upon the ark of the testimony, I will speak with you of all that I will give you in commandment for the people of Israel."

[Ex 25:21-22]

Let us then with confidence draw near to the throne of grace, that we may receive mercy and find grace to help in time of need.

[Heb 4:16]

"As the Father has loved me, so have I loved you; abide in my love."

[Jn 15:9]

"I have loved you with an everlasting love…."

[Jer 31:3]

"I am the vine, you are the branches. He who abides in me, and I in him, he it is that bears much fruit, for apart from me you can do nothing."

[Jn 15:5]

And the Word became flesh and dwelt among us....

[Jn 1:14]

"For where two or three are gathered in my name, there am I in the midst of them."

[Mt 18:20]

"... And I, when I am lifted up from the earth, will draw all men to myself."

[Jn 12:32]

"For this I was born, and for this I have come into the world, to bear witness to the truth. Everyone who is of the truth hears my voice."

[Jn 18:37]

But one of the soldiers pierced his side with a spear, and at once there came out blood and water.

[Jn 19:34]

"... Lo, I am with you always, to the close of the age."

[Mt 28:20]

REFLECTIONS ON EUCHARISTIC DEVOTION FROM THE POPES AND CHURCH DOCUMENTS

POPE JOHN XXIII ON BENEDICTION

This may be called the evening sacrifice, because Benediction is generally in the evening, while the Holy Mass, at least according to the custom which prevailed until a short time ago, was always celebrated in the morning hours.

St. Philip Neri, in an ecstasy during Benediction, saw in the Sacred Host a crowd of kneeling people and Jesus blessing them, as if this were his usual habit, the customary expression of his kindness shown in the Blessed Sacrament.

Oh what graces Jesus, ever present with us, showers upon us during Benediction! From my earliest childhood I was taught to make the sign of the cross three times when the priest blessed us with the holy monstrance.

In fact, in the Gospel Jesus is seen three times in the act of blessing. He blessed the children; he blessed the bread and the cup at the Last Supper; he blessed his disciples when he was about to leave them and ascend to heaven, as a pledge of the great blessing they would receive at the Last Judgment.

The eucharistic blessing shows us how close Jesus is to us in our humble lives. "God with us." His blessing falls upon our troubles and afflictions, our anxieties and temptations, our failings and weaknesses, which in that moment we do not try to hide from him, and also upon all the frailties of our spirit, upon circumstances the dangers of which are not yet apparent to us; upon the evil spirits who try to scare and bewilder us; and upon our beloved and faithful Guardian Angels, as if to reward them for their loving care.[49]

MYSTERIUM FIDEI, 1965
POPE PAUL VI

In the course of the day the faithful should not omit to visit the Blessed Sacrament, which according to the liturgical laws must be kept in the churches with great reverence in a most honorable location. Such visits are a proof of gratitude, an expression of love, an acknowledgment of the Lord's presence.[50]

But there is yet another manner in which Christ

is present in His Church, a manner which surpasses all the others; it is His presence in the Sacrament of the Eucharist, which is for this reason "a more consoling source of devotion, a more lovely object of contemplation, a more effective means of sanctification than all the other sacraments." The reason is clear; it contains Christ Himself....[51]

However, venerable brothers, in this very matter which we are discussing, there are not lacking reasons for serious pastoral concern and anxiety. The awareness of our apostolic duty does not allow us to be silent in the face of these problems. Indeed, we are aware of the fact that, among those who deal with this Most Holy Mystery in written or spoken word, there are some who, with reference either to Masses which are celebrated in private, or to the dogma of transubstantiation, or to devotion to the Eucharist, spread abroad opinions which disturb the faithful and fill their minds with no little confusion about matters of faith. It is as if everyone were permitted to consign to oblivion doctrine already defined by the Church, or else to interpret it in such a way as to weaken the genuine meaning of the words or the recognized force of the concepts involved.

To confirm what we have said by examples, it is not allowable to emphasize what is called the "communal" Mass to the disparagement of Masses celebrated in private, or to exaggerate the element of sacramental sign as if the symbolism, which all certainly admit in the Eucharist, expresses fully and exhausts completely the mode of Christ's presence in this sacrament. Nor is it allowable to discuss the mystery of transubstantiation without mentioning what the Council of Trent stated about the marvelous conversion of the whole substance of the bread into the Body and of the whole substance of the wine into the Blood of Christ, speaking rather only of what is called "transignification" and "transfiguration," or finally to propose and act upon the opinion according to which, in the Consecrated Hosts which remain after the celebration of the sacrifice of the Mass, Christ Our Lord is no longer present.

Everyone can see that the spread of these and similar opinions does great harm to the faith and devotion to the Divine Eucharist.

And therefore, so that the hope aroused by the council, that a flourishing of eucharistic piety which is now pervading the whole Church, be not frustrated by this spread of false opinions, we have with apostolic authority decided to address you, venerable brothers, and to express our mind on this subject.

We certainly do not wish to deny in those who are spreading these singular opinions the praiseworthy effort to investigate this lofty mystery and to set forth its inexhaustible riches, revealing its meaning to the men of today; rather we acknowledge and approve their effort. However, we cannot approve the opinions which they express, and we have the duty to warn you about the grave danger which these opinions involve for correct faith.[52]

St. John Chrysostom, who, as you know, treated of the eucharistic mystery with such nobility of language and insight born of devotion, instructing his faithful on one occasion about this mystery, expressed these most fitting words: "Let us submit to God in all things and not contradict Him, even if what He says seems contrary to our reason and intellect; rather let His words prevail over our reason and intellect. Let us act in this way with regard to the (eucharistic) mysteries, looking not only at what falls under our senses but holding on to His words. For His word cannot lead us astray."

The scholastic Doctors often made similar affirmations: That in this sacrament are the true Body of Christ and His true Blood is something that "cannot be apprehended by the senses," says St. Thomas, "but only by faith which relies on divine authority. This is why, in a comment on Luke 22:19 ('This is My Body which is given for you'), St. Cyril says: 'Do not doubt whether this is true, but rather receive the words of the Savior in faith, for since He is the truth, He cannot lie.'"

Thus the Christian people, echoing the words of the same St. Thomas, frequently sing the words: "Sight, touch, and taste in Thee are each deceived, the ear alone most safely is believed. I believe all the Son of God has spoken — than truth's own word there is no truer token."

In fact, St. Bonaventure asserts: "There is no difficulty about Christ's presence in the Eucharist as in a sign, but that He is truly present in the Eucharist as He is in heaven, this is most difficult. Therefore to believe this is especially meritorious."

Moreover, the Holy Gospel alludes to this when it tells of the many disciples of Christ who, after listening to the sermon about eating His Flesh and drinking His Blood, turned away and left Our Lord, saying: "This is strange talk, who can be expected to listen to it?" Peter, on the other hand, in reply to Jesus' question whether also the twelve wished to leave, expressed his faith and that of the others promptly and resolutely with the marvelous answer: "Lord, to whom should we go? Thy words are the words of eternal life."[53]

The Catholic Church has always offered and still offers the cult of Latria to the Sacrament of the Eucharist, not only during Mass, but also outside of it, reserving Consecrated Hosts with the utmost care, exposing them to solemn veneration, and carrying them processionally to the joy of great crowds of the faithful.[54]

"CREDO" OF THE PEOPLE OF GOD, 1968
POPE PAUL VI

The unique and indivisible existence of the Lord glorious in Heaven is not multiplied, but is rendered present by the Sacrament in the many places on earth where Mass is celebrated. And this existence remains present, after the Sacrifice, in the Blessed Sacrament which is, in the tabernacle, the living heart of each of our churches. And it is our very sweet duty to honour and adore in the Blessed Host which our eyes see, the Incarnate Word Whom they cannot see, and Who, without leaving Heaven, is made present before us.[55]

EUCHARISTIAE SACRAMENTUM, 1973
(SACRED CONGREGATION FOR DIVINE WORSHIP)

There can accordingly be no doubt "that all the faithful ought to show to this most holy sacrament the worship which is due to the true God, as has always been the custom of the Catholic Church. Nor is it to be adored any the less because it was instituted by Christ the Lord to be eaten."[56]

AT THE PARIS BASILICA OF THE SACRED HEART, MONTMARTRE, A SHRINE OF PERPETUAL ADORATION, JUNE 1, 1980
POPE JOHN PAUL II

We are called not only to meditate on, and contemplate, this mystery of Christ's love; we are called to take part in it. It is the mystery of the Holy Eucharist, the centre of our faith, the centre of our worship of Christ's merciful love manifested in his Sacred Heart, a mystery which is adored here night and day, in this basilica, which thereby becomes one of these centres from which the Lord's love and grace radiate in a mysterious but real way on your city, on your country and on the redeemed world....

In the Holy Eucharist — this is also the meaning of perpetual worship — we enter this movement of love from which all interior progress and all apostolic efficacy springs: "and I, when I am lifted up from the earth, will draw all men to myself" (Jn 12:32).[57]

ON THE FEAST OF CORPUS CHRISTI, 1979
POPE JOHN PAUL II

Let us remember that the place of Christ's presence on earth was not only the Upper Room in

Jerusalem, but also the streets of towns and country roads. Everywhere people gathered before him. They gathered together to be able to be with him, to listen to him.

In the solemnity of Corpus Christi this particular presence of Christ in the streets, squares, and by the wayside, is reserved. He speaks to us who have gathered, not with the living words of the Gospel, as he once did, but with the eloquent silence of the Eucharist.

In this silence of the white Host, carried in the ostensory [monstrance], are all his words; there is his whole life given in offering to the Father for each of us; there is also the glory of the glorified body, which started with the resurrection, and still continues in heavenly union.[58]

DOMINICAE CENAE, 1980
POPE JOHN PAUL II

The Church and the world have a great need for Eucharistic worship. Jesus awaits us in this sacrament of love. Let us not refuse the time to go to meet him in adoration, in contemplation full of faith, and open to making amends for the serious offenses and crimes of the world. Let our adoration never cease.[59]

GENERAL AUDIENCE, JUNE 13, 1979
POPE JOHN PAUL II

"Lord, you know that I love you ... Lord, you know that I love you" (Jn 21:15-17). The Eucharist is, in a certain way, the culminating point of this answer. I wish to repeat it together with the whole Church to Him, who manifested his love by means of the Sacrament of His Body and Blood, remaining with us "to the close of the age" (Mt 28:20).[60]

REDEMPTOR HOMINIS, 1979
POPE JOHN PAUL II

The Eucharist is the center and summit of the whole of sacramental life, through which each Christian receives the saving power of the Redemption, beginning with the mystery of Baptism, in which we are buried into the death of Christ, in order to become sharers in his Resurrection, as the Apostle teaches (cf. Rom 6:3-5). In the light of this teaching, we see still more clearly the reason why the entire sacramental life of the Church and of each Christian reaches its summit and fullness in the Eucharist.[61]

LETTER TO THE BISHOP OF LIÈGE IN COMMEMORATION OF THE 750TH ANNIVERSARY OF THE FIRST CELEBRATION OF THE FEAST OF CORPUS CHRISTI, MAY 28, 1996

POPE JOHN PAUL II

Outside the Eucharistic celebration, the Church is careful to venerate the Blessed Sacrament, which must be "reserved ... as the spiritual centre of the religious and parish community" (Paul VI, *Mysterium fidei*, n. 68). Contemplation prolongs Communion and enables one to meet Christ, true God and true man, in a lasting way, to let oneself be seen by him and to experience his presence. When we contemplate him present in the Blessed Sacrament of the altar, Christ draws near to us and becomes more intimate to us than we are to ourselves. He grants us a share in his divine life in a transforming union and, in the Spirit, he gives us access to the Father, as he himself said to Philip: "He who has seen me has seen the Father" (Jn 14:9)....

I urge priests, religious and lay people to continue and redouble their efforts to teach the younger generations the meaning and value of Eucharistic adoration and devotion. How will young people be able to know the Lord if they are not introduced to the mystery of his presence? Like the young Samuel, by learning the

95

words of the prayer of the heart, they will be closer to the Lord, who will accompany them in their spiritual and human growth, and in the missionary witness which they must give throughout their life.[62]

CODE OF CANON LAW, 1983

Christ's faithful are to hold the blessed Eucharist in the highest honour. They should take an active part in the celebration of the most august Sacrifice of the Mass; they should receive the sacrament with great devotion and frequently, and should reverence it with the greatest adoration. In explaining the doctrine of this sacrament, pastors of souls are assiduously to instruct the faithful about their obligation in this regard.[63]

CATECHISM OF THE CATHOLIC CHURCH, 1994

It is for this reason that the tabernacle should be located in an especially worthy place in the church and should be constructed in such a way that it emphasizes and manifests the truth of the real presence of Christ in the Blessed Sacrament.

It is highly fitting that Christ should have wanted to remain present to his Church in this unique way. Since Christ was about to take his departure from his own in his visible form, he wanted to give us his sacramental presence; since he was about to offer himself on the cross to save us, he wanted us to have the memorial of the love with which he loved us "to the end" ....[64]

APPENDIX A: INDULGENCES FOR EUCHARISTIC DEVOTION

FROM THE *ENCHIRIDION* OF *INDULGENCES*, 1968
POPE PAUL VI

A *partial indulgence* is granted to the faithful, who visit the Most Blessed Sacrament to adore it; a plenary indulgence is granted, if the visit lasts for at least one half an hour. [*Enchiridion of Indulgences*, Adoratio Ss.mi Sacramenti][65]

To be capable of gaining an indulgence for oneself, it is required that one be baptized, not excommunicated, in the state of grace at least at the completion of the prescribed works, and a subject of the one granting the indulgence.

In order that one who is capable may actually gain indulgences, one must have at least a general intention to gain them and must in accordance with the tenor of the grant perform the enjoined works at the time and in the manner prescribed....

To acquire a plenary indulgence it is necessary to perform the work to which the indulgence is attached and to fulfill the following three conditions:

sacramental confession, eucharistic Communion, and prayer for the intention of the Sovereign Pontiff. It is further required that all attachment to sin, even venial sin, be absent....

The three conditions may be fulfilled several days before or after the performance of the prescribed work; it is, however, fitting that Communion be received and the prayer for the intention of the Sovereign Pontiff be said on the same day the work is performed....

The condition of praying for the intention of the Sovereign Pontiff is fully satisfied by reciting one *Our Father* and one *Hail Mary*; nevertheless, each one is free to recite any other prayer according to his piety and devotion [*Enchiridion of Indulgences*, "Norms on Indulgences" nos. 22, 26, 27, 29].[66]

APPENDIX B: OTHER PRAYERS OF THE CHURCH

(FROM THE CURRENT ENCHIRIDION OF INDULGENCES)

AN ACT OF SPIRITUAL COMMUNION

My Jesus, I believe that you are in the Blessed Sacrament. I love you above all things, and I long for you in my soul. Since I cannot now receive you sacramentally, come at least spiritually into my heart. As though you have already come, I embrace you and unite myself entirely to you; never permit me to be separated from you.[67]

LITANY OF THE MOST SACRED HEART OF JESUS

Lord, have mercy.
Christ, have mercy.
Lord, have mercy.
Christ, hear us.
Christ, graciously hear us.
God, the Father of Heaven, have mercy on us.*

[*Have mercy on us* is repeated after each
   invocation.]

God the Son, Redeemer of the world,

God, the Holy Spirit,

Holy Trinity, One God,

Heart of Jesus, Son of the Eternal Father,

Heart of Jesus, formed by the Holy Spirit in the
   womb of the Virgin Mother,

Heart of Jesus, substantially united to the Word
   of God,

Heart of Jesus, of Infinite Majesty,

Heart of Jesus, Sacred Temple of God,

Heart of Jesus, Tabernacle of the Most High,

Heart of Jesus, House of God and Gate of Heaven,

Heart of Jesus, burning furnace of charity,

Heart of Jesus, abode of justice and love,

Heart of Jesus, full of goodness and love,

Heart of Jesus, abyss of all virtues,

Heart of Jesus, most worthy of all praise,

Heart of Jesus, king and center of all hearts,

Heart of Jesus, in whom are all the treasures of
   wisdom and knowledge,

Heart of Jesus, in whom dwells the fullness of
   divinity,

Heart of Jesus, in whom the Father was well
   pleased,

Heart of Jesus, of whose fullness we have all
   received,

Heart of Jesus, desire of the everlasting hills,
Heart of Jesus, patient and most merciful,
Heart of Jesus, enriching all who invoke you,
Heart of Jesus, fountain of life and holiness,
Heart of Jesus, propitiation for our sins,
Heart of Jesus, loaded down with opprobrium,
Heart of Jesus, bruised for our offenses,
Heart of Jesus, obedient to death,
Heart of Jesus, pierced with a lance,
Heart of Jesus, source of all consolation,
Heart of Jesus, our life and resurrection,
Heart of Jesus, our peace and reconciliation,
Heart of Jesus, victim for our sins,
Heart of Jesus, salvation of those who trust in
    you,
Heart of Jesus, hope of those who die in you,
Heart of Jesus, delight of all the Saints,
Lamb of God, who take away the sins of the world,
    spare us, O Lord.
Lamb of God, who take away the sins of the world,
    graciously hear us, *O Lord.*
Lamb of God, who take away the sins of the world,
    have mercy on us.

V. Jesus, meek and humble of heart.
R. Make our hearts like to yours.
Let us pray.

Almighty and eternal God, look upon the Heart of your most beloved Son and upon the praises and satisfaction which he offers you in the name of sinners; and to those who implore your mercy, in your great goodness, grant forgiveness in the name of the same Jesus Christ, your Son, who lives and reigns with you forever and ever. R. Amen.[68]

LITANY OF THE MOST HOLY NAME OF JESUS

Lord, have mercy.

Christ, have mercy.

Lord, have mercy.

Jesus, hear us.

Jesus, graciously hear us.

God, the Father of Heaven, *have mercy on us*.*

[*Have mercy on us* is repeated after each
 invocation down to *Jesus, Crown of all Saints*.]

God the Son, Redeemer of the world,

God, the Holy Spirit,

Holy Trinity, one God,

Jesus, Son of the living God,

Jesus, Splendor of the Father,

Jesus, Brightness of eternal Light,

Jesus, King of Glory,

Jesus, Sun of Justice,

Jesus, Son of the Virgin Mary,
Jesus, most amiable,
Jesus, most admirable,
Jesus, the mighty God,
Jesus, Father of the world to come,
Jesus, angel of great counsel,
Jesus, most powerful,
Jesus, most patient,
Jesus, most obedient,
Jesus, meek and humble of heart,
Jesus, Lover of Chastity,
Jesus, our Lover,
Jesus, God of Peace,
Jesus, Author of Life,
Jesus, Model of Virtues,
Jesus, zealous for souls,
Jesus, our God,
Jesus, our Refuge,
Jesus, Father of the Poor,
Jesus, Treasure of the Faithful,
Jesus, good Shepherd,
Jesus, true Light,
Jesus, eternal Wisdom,
Jesus, infinite Goodness,
Jesus, our Way and our Life,
Jesus, joy of the Angels,
Jesus, King of the Patriarchs,
Jesus, Master of the Apostles,

Jesus, Teacher of the Evangelists,
Jesus, Strength of Martyrs,
Jesus, Light of Confessors,
Jesus, Purity of Virgins,
Jesus, Crown of all Saints,
Be merciful, *spare us, O Jesus*!
Be merciful, *graciously hear us, O Jesus*!
From all evil, *deliver us, O Jesus.**
[**Deliver us, O Jesus*, is repeated after each
    invocation down to *Through your Glory*.]
From all sin,
From your wrath,
From the snares of the devil,
From the spirit of fornication,
From everlasting death,
From the neglect of your inspirations,
Through the mystery of your holy Incarnation,
Through your Nativity,
Through your Infancy,
Through your most divine Life,
Through your Labors,
Through your Agony and Passion,
Through your Cross and Dereliction,
Through your Sufferings,
Through your Death and Burial,
Through your Resurrection,
Through your Ascension,

Through your Institution of the Most Holy
    Eucharist,
Through your Joys,
Through your Glory,
Lamb of God, who take away the sins of the world,
    spare us, O Jesus!
Lamb of God, who take away the sins of the world,
    graciously hear us, O Jesus!
Lamb of God, who take away the sins of the world,
    have mercy on us, O Jesus!
Jesus, hear us.
    Jesus, graciously hear us.

Let us pray.

O Lord Jesus Christ, you have said, "Ask and you shall receive; seek, and you shall find; knock, and it shall be opened to you"; mercifully attend to our supplications, and grant us the grace of your most divine love, that we may love you with all our hearts, and in all our words and actions, and never cease to praise you.

Make us, O Lord, to have a perpetual fear and love of your holy name, for you never fail to govern those whom you solidly establish in your love. You, who live and reign forever and ever. R. Amen.[69]

POSTSCRIPT

PRAYER FOR THE SPREAD OF PERPETUAL EUCHARISTIC ADORATION

Heavenly Father, increase our faith in the Real Presence of Your Son, Jesus Christ in the Holy Eucharist. We are obliged to adore Him, to give Him thanks and to make reparation for sins. We need Your peace in our hearts and among nations. We need conversion from our sins and the mercy of Your forgiveness. May we obtain this through prayer and our union with the Eucharistic Lord. Please send down the Holy Spirit upon all peoples to give them the love, courage, strength and willingness to respond to the invitation to Perpetual Eucharistic Adoration.

We beseech You to spread perpetual exposition of the Most Blessed Sacrament in parishes around the world.

We ask this in the name of Jesus the Lord.

Amen.

Our Lady of the Most Blessed Sacrament help us to spread the glory of Your Son through perpetual exposition of the Holy Eucharist.[70]

PRAYER TO OUR LADY
OF THE BLESSED SACRAMENT

O Virgin Mary, our Lady of the Blessed Sacrament, glory of the Christian people, joy of the universal Church, salvation of the world; pray for us, and awaken in all the faithful devotion to the Holy Eucharist in order that they render themselves worthy to receive it daily.[71]

Sources for Prayer Texts

Note: There are many great Eucharistic prayers not given in this booklet. This is only an introduction. Further reading and references to prayers can be found in the work In *the Presence of our Lord: The History, Theology and Psychology of Eucharistic Devotion*, by Father Benedict J. Groeschel, C.F.R., and James Monti (Huntington, IN: Our Sunday Visitor; Steubenville, OH: Franciscan University Press, 1997).

1. St. Teresa of Ávila, *The Way of Perfection*, trans. E. Allison Peers (Garden City, New York: Image Books/Doubleday and Co., Inc., 1964), chap. 34, p. 227.

2. Fr. Benedict J. Groeschel, C.F.R., and James Monti, *In the Presence of Our Lord: The History, Theology an Psychology of Eucharistic Devotion* (Huntington, IN: Our Sunday Visitor, 1997), pp. 42-43, 44-46, 99-100, 179, 180.

3. Ibid., pp. 193-198, 279.

4. Ibid., pp. 121-125, 209-225.

5. *Meditations on Mary: Conferences by the Servant*

of God Terence Cardinal Cooke, intro. by Fr. Benedict J. Groeschel, C.F.R. (Staten Island, NY: Alba House, 1993), pp. 79, 80.

6. From "Letter to a General Chapter," in Regis J. Armstrong, O.F.M. Cap., *St. Francis of Assisi: Writings for a Gospel Life* (New York: Crossroad Publishing Co., 1994), pp. 218-219.

7. Thomas à Kempis, *My Imitation of Christ: Revised Translation* (Brooklyn: Confraternity of the Precious Blood, 1954), bk. 4, ch. 3, pp. 396-398.

8. *Excerpted from Preparing Yourself for Mass* by Romano Guardini (Matthias Grunewald Verlay, 1939). English Translation by Sophia Institute (Manchester, NH: Sophia Institute Press, 1993), pp. 176-177.

9. Bishop Jacob Aphraates, *On Fasting*, in Fr. J. Simon, O.S.M., "Syrian Eucharistica," *Homiletic and Pastoral Review*, 21 (May 1921), p. 696.

10. Translated from Latin text in *Acta Sanctorum*, May, Tome 4 (rpt., Paris: Victor Palme, 1866), p. 69 (no. 92).

11. *The Divine Liturgy of Our Father Saint John Chrysostom* (Pittsburgh: Byzantine Seminary

Press, 1965), p. 28.

12. Ven. John Henry Newman, *Prayers, Verses, and Devotions* (rpt., San Francisco: Ignatius Press, 1989), pp. 423-424.

13. *Ancient Devotions for Holy Communion* (London: Burns, Oates & Washbourne, Ltd., 1948), pp. 35-36 (English modernized).

14. Sr. Benedicta Ward, S.L.G., *The Prayers and Meditations of St. Anselm* (London: Penguin Books, 1973), pp. 100-101.

15. William Maskell, ed., *Monumenta Ritualia Ecclesiae Anglicanae: The Occasional Offices of the Church of England according to the Old Use of Salisbury, the Prymer in English and Other Prayers and Forms with Dissertations and Notes* (Oxford: Clarendon Press, 1882), vol. 3, p. 283 (English modernized).

16. Robert Van de Weyer, ed., *The Harper Collins Book of Prayers: A Treasury of Prayers through the Ages* (San Francisco: Harper Collins, 1993), p. 26.
17. Frederick E. Warren, trans., *The Sarum Missal in English* (1526 edition), The Library of Litur-

giology & Ecclesiology for English Readers, vol. 8 (London: Alexander Moring Ltd., 1911), Part I, p. 18 (English modernized). For attribution to St. Thomas Aquinas, see William Bright, *Ancient Collects and other Prayers* (Oxford: Parker and Co., 1887), p. 138, note.

18. From the "Latin-prayers" Internet website of Michael Martin.

19. Letter to Padre Agostino, April 18, 1912, in Venerable Padre Pio, *Letters: Vol. I: Correspondence with His Spiritual Directors (1910-1922),* ed. Melchiorre of Pobladura and Alessandro of Ripabottoni (San Giovanni Rotondo, Italy: Editions "Padre Pio da Pietrelcina," 1985), p. 308.

20. *Autobiography,* chap. 38, no. 21, in *The Collected Works of St. Teresa of Ávila: Volume One*, trans. Kieran Kavanaugh, O.C.D., and Otilio Rodriguez, O.C.D. (Washington, D.C.: ICS Publications, 1976), Vol. 1, p. 263.

21. Text provided by Father Benedict J. Groeschel, C.F.R.

22. Abridged and adapted with modifications from text in Raymond E.F. Larsson, ed., *Saints at*

Prayer (*New York: Coward-McCann, Inc.*, 1942), pp. 131-132.

23. Excerpted from text in A. Hamman, O.F.M., ed., *Early Christian Prayers* (Chicago: Henry Regnery Co.; London: Longmans, Green, 1961), pp. 140-141.

24. Text in Fr. Nicholas Caussin, S.J., *The Holy Court* (London: W. Bentley, 1650), p. 464 (English modernized).

25. Newman, *Prayers, Verses, and Devotions*, p. 314.

26. Text in *Works of Love Are Works of Peace: Mother Teresa of Calcutta and the Missionaries of Charity,* photographs by Michael Collopy (San Francisco: Ignatius Press, 1996), pp. 202-203, adapted from the text of Cardinal Newman, *Meditations on Christian Doctrine*, VII, no. 3, 3, in Newman, *Prayers, Verses, and Devotions*, pp. 389-390.

27. Text in Fr. Matthew Britt, O.S.B., ed., *The Hymns of the Breviary and Missal* (New York: Benziger Brothers, 1922), p. 192.

28. In F. A. Gasquet, ed., *Ancestral Prayers* (Springfield, IL: Templegate Publishers, 1996), pp. 58-60

(English modernized).

29. Prayer 10, in Sr. Suzanne Noffke, O.P., ed., *The Prayers of Catherine of Siena* (New York: Paulist Press, 1983), pp. 78-79 (qtd. with slight modification).

30. From the 1841 Armenian liturgy translation of John Mason Neale in E.F.K. Fortescue, *The Armenian Church* (London: J.T. Hayes, 1872; rpt. New York: AMS Press, Inc., 1970), pp. 105-106 (English modernized).

31. Fr. Stefano M. Manelli, F.F.I., *Jesus Our Eucharistic Love: Eucharistic Life Exemplified by the Saints* (New Bedford, NH: Franciscan Friars of the Immaculate, 1996), pp. 100-101.

32. From Neale translation in Fortescue, pp. 108-109 (English modernized).

33. James Patrick Derum, *The Porter of Saint Bonaventure's: The Life of Father Solanus Casey, Capuchin* (Detroit: The Fidelity Press, 1972), p. 248.

34. St. Peter Julian Eymard, *Eucharistic Handbook*, Eymard Library, Vol. 6 (New York: Eymard

League, 1948), p. 209.

35. Newman, *Prayers, Verses, and Devotions*, p. 335.

36. Adapted with modifications from *A Christian's Rule of Life,* in St. Alphonsus Liguori, *The Way of Salvation, to which is added A Christian's Rule of Life* (New York: Catholic Book Publishing Co., 1948), pp. 267-268.

37. Excerpted from text in St. Thérèse of Lisieux, *The Poetry of Saint Thérèse of Lisieux*, trans. Donald Kinney, O.C.D. (Washington, D.C.: ICS Publications, 1996), pp. 89, 90, 92, verses 1, 3, 4, 12.

38. From *Daily Bulletins of the Ufficio stampa Vaticana*, 24 Jan. 1959, in John Donnelly, ed., Prayers and Devotions from Pope John XXIII (New York: Grosset & Dunlap, Inc., 1967), pp. 92-93.

39. Excerpted from "'Lord, stay with us!': Pope John Paul's Prayer in the Blessed Sacrament Chapel," Dec. 2, 1981, *L'Osservatore Romano,* Dec. 14, 1981, pp. 10-11.

40. *Works of Love Are Works of Peace*, p. 203.
41. Text in Van de Weyer, p. 110.

42. St. John Eudes, *Meditations on Various Subjects* (New York: P.J. Kenedy & Sons, 1947), p. 35 (English modernized).

43. "A Devout Prayer," in Garry Haupt, ed., *Treatise on the Passion; Treatise on the Blessed Body; Instructions and Prayers*, Complete Works of St. Thomas More, vol. 13 (New Haven: Yale University Press, 1976), p. 230 (English modernized).

44. Translated from Spanish text in P. Fausto Casa, *Los Primeros Viernes* (Buenos Aires, Argentina: Editorial Claretiana, 1985), pp. 106-107.

45. Text in *Roman Breviary in English: Autumn*, ed. Rt. Rev. Msgr. Joseph A. Nelson, D.D. (New York: Benziger Brothers, Inc., 1950), pp. 14**-15**.

46. Excerpted from text in Britt, p. 183, verses 1, 3, 5.

47. Excerpted from text in Robert Anderson and Johann Moser, trans. and ed., *Devoutly I Adore Thee: The Prayers and Hymns of St. Thomas Aquinas* (Manchester, NH: Sophia Institute Press, 1993), pp. 101, 103, 109, verses 1, 2, 11, 23, 24.

48. From Homily for Eucharistic Procession, Cremona, Italy, June 21, 1992, *L'Osservatore Romano*,

July 15, 1992, p. 6, no. 7.

49. *Scritti e Discorsi III*, in Donnelly, p. 100.

50. Pope Paul VI, *Encyclical Letter of His Holiness Pope Paul VI: Mystery of Faith: Mysterium Fidei*, Sept. 3, 1965 (Boston: St. Paul Editions, n.d.), p. 26.

51. Ibid., p. 17.

52. Ibid., pp. 7-8.

53. Ibid., pp. 9-10.

54. Ibid., p. 23.

55. Pope Paul VI, *The "Credo" of the People of God*, June 30, 1968, Tipografia Poliglotta Vaticana edition (distributed by: New Rochelle, NY: Catholics United for the Faith, Inc., n.d.), p. 19.

56. Sacred Congregation for Divine Worship, *Eucharistiae Sacramentum*, June 21, 1973, no. 3 (citing Eucharisticum mysterium, no. 3), in Fr. Austin Flannery, O.P., ed., *Vatican Council II: The Conciliar and Post Conciliar Documents* (Northport, NY: Costello Publishing Co., 1975),

p. 243.

57. Pope John Paul II, Meditation at the Basilica of Montmartre, June 1, 1980, *L'Osservatore Romano*, June 16, 1980, p. 15, no. 4.

58. Pope John Paul II, Angelus Address, June 17, 1979, *L'Osservatore Romano*, June 25, 1979, p. 2, no. 1.

59. Pope John Paul II, *Dominicae Cenae*, no. 3, 1980, Vatican Press, Rome.

60. Pope John Paul II, Address at the General Audience, June 13, 1979, *L'Osservatore Romano*, June 18, 1979, p. 12.

61. Pope John Paul II, *Redemptor Hominis*, March 4, 1979, in *The Encyclicals of John Paul II*, J. Michael Miller, C.S.B., ed. (Our Sunday Visitor: Huntington, IN, 1996), p. 85, no. 20.1.

62. Letter to the Bishop of Liège Albert Houssiau, May 28, 1996, in *L'Osservatore Romano*, June 26, 1996, p. 6, nos. 3, 8.

63. *Code of Canon Law*, Jan. 25, 1983, Canon 898, in Canon Law Society of Great Britain and Ireland,

ed., *The Code of Canon Law* (London: Collins/William B. Eerdmans Publishing Co., 1983), p. 165.

64. *Catechism of the Catholic Church*, English edition (Libreria Editrice Vaticana, 1994), nos. 1379-1380, p. 348.

65. *Enchiridion of Endulgences: Norms and Grants*, trans. William T. Barry, C.SS.R. (New York: Catholic Book Publishing Co., 1969), "Other Grants of Indulgences," p. 46.

66. Ibid., *Norms on Indulgences*, pp. 25-26.

67. In "English Supplement" to ibid., p. 116.

68. Ibid., pp. 118-119.

69. Ibid., pp. 116-118.

70. From *Eucharistic Holy Hour* (Los Angeles: Perpetual Eucharistic Adoration, 1987), p. 5.

71. Ibid., p. 4.

INDEX OF AUTHORS CITED

Paul VI, Pope
Symeon, St. (tenth century)
Teresa of Ávila, St.
Thérèse of Lisieux, St.
Thomas à Kempis